Shark Bites

Blue Shark

by Jenna Lee Gleisner

Bullfrog Books

Ideas for Parents and Teachers

Bullfrog Books let children practice reading informational text at the earliest reading levels. Repetition, familiar words, and photo labels support early readers.

Before Reading

- Discuss the cover photo. What does it tell them?

- Look at the picture glossary together. Read and discuss the words.

Read the Book

- "Walk" through the book and look at the photos. Let the child ask questions. Point out the photo labels.

- Read the book to the child, or have him or her read independently.

After Reading

- Prompt the child to think more. Ask: Blue sharks swim near the surface. Their fins can often be seen rising out of the water. Would you want to see one?

Bullfrog Books are published by Jump!
5357 Penn Avenue South
Minneapolis, MN 55419
www.jumplibrary.com

Library of Congress Cataloging-in-Publication Data

Names: Gleisner, Jenna Lee, author.
Title: Blue shark / by Jenna Lee Gleisner.
Description: Bullfrog books edition.
Minneapolis, MN: Jump!, Inc., [2020]
Series: Shark bites
Includes bibliographical references and index.
Audience: Age 5-8. | Audience: K to Grade 3.
Identifiers: LCCN 2019001173 (print)
LCCN 2019002851 (ebook)
ISBN 9781641289580 (ebook)
ISBN 9781641289573 (hardcover : alk. paper)
Subjects: LCSH: Blue shark—Juvenile literature.
Classification: LCC QL638.95.C3 (ebook)
LCC QL638.95.C3 G54 2020 (print)
DDC 597.3/4—dc23
LC record available at https://lccn.loc.gov/2019001173

Editors: Susanne Bushman and Jenna Trnka
Design: Shoreline Publishing Group

Photo Credits: Martin Prochazkacz/Shutterstock, cover, 24; Morethanalegend/Shutterstock, 1; Ethan Daniels/Dreamstime, 3; Shane Gross/Shutterstock, 4; Vpommeyrol, 5, 23bl; Nature Picture Library/Alamy, 6–7, 14–15; Erik Schlogl/Alamy, 8–9; Wildestanimal/Shutterstock, 10–11, 23br; Maieru Alina/Dreamstime, 12, 23tr; Cultura Creative/Alamy, 13; Nature Picture Library/Getty, 16–17; Musat Christian/Dreamstime, 18; Ramon Carretero/Dreamstime, 19; Joost van Uffelen/Shutterstock, 20–21; Marion Kraschi/Shutterstock, 22, 23tl.

Printed in the United States of America at Corporate Graphics in North Mankato, Minnesota.

Table of Contents

A shark swims.

Where?

Near the surface.

It is slim.

It is a blue shark!

It is blue.

Like its name!

fin

It has a white belly.
And long fins.

See its snout?

It is long.

Its shape and size
helps it swim.

It cuts through
the water.

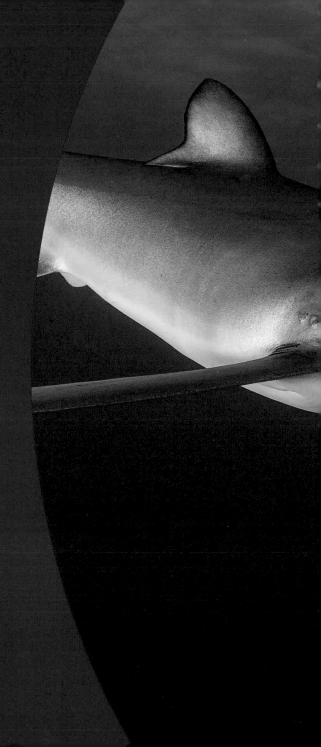

snout

It looks for prey.
Like what?
Octopus. Squid.

squid

12

Fish. Lobsters. Crabs, too.

Cool!

13

Blue sharks
gang up.

Why?

To hunt in a group!

Wow!

orca
whale

18

Larger sharks.

great
white
shark

This shark is agile!

It gets away!

Nice!

Parts of a Blue Shark

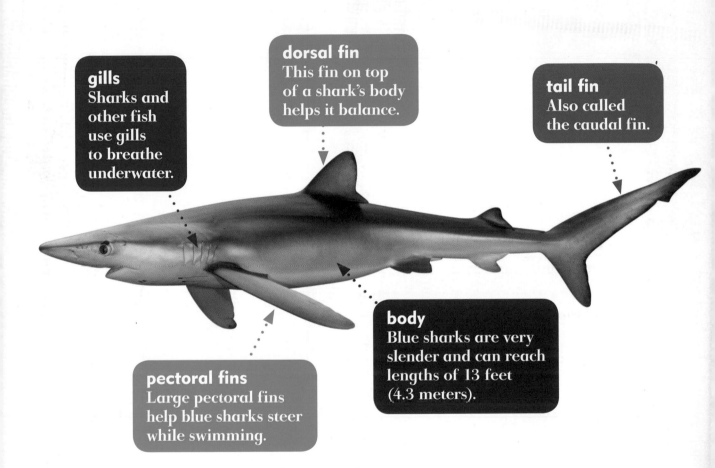

gills
Sharks and other fish use gills to breathe underwater.

dorsal fin
This fin on top of a shark's body helps it balance.

tail fin
Also called the caudal fin.

body
Blue sharks are very slender and can reach lengths of 13 feet (4.3 meters).

pectoral fins
Large pectoral fins help blue sharks steer while swimming.

Picture Glossary

agile
Having the ability to move quickly and with grace.

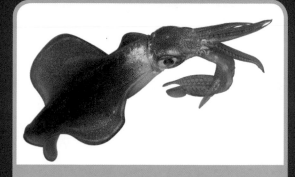

prey
Animals that are hunted by other animals for food.

slim
Thin and graceful.

snout
The long front part of an animal's head that includes the nose, mouth, and jaws.

Index

To Learn More

Finding more information is as easy as 1, 2, 3.

① Go to www.factsurfer.com

② Enter "blueshark" into the search box.

③ Choose your book to see a list of websites.